Who Was Jane Austen?

by Sarah Fabiny

illustrated by Jerry Hoare

Penguin Workshop
An Imprint of Penguin Random House

For my mom, who taught me "there is no enjoyment like reading!"—SF

PENGUIN WORKSHOP
Penguin Young Readers Group
An Imprint of Penguin Random House LLC

Text copyright © 2017 by Sarah Fabiny. Illustrations copyright © 2017 by Penguin Random House LLC. All rights reserved. Published by Penguin Workshop, an imprint of Penguin Random House LLC, 345 Hudson Street, New York, New York 10014. PENGUIN and PENGUIN WORKSHOP are trademarks of Penguin Books Ltd. WHO HQ & Design is a registered trademark of Penguin Random House LLC. Printed in the USA.

Library of Congress Cataloging-in-Publication Data is available.

ISBN 9780448488639 (paperback)   10 9 8 7 6 5 4 3 2 1
ISBN 9780515157994 (library binding)   10 9 8 7 6 5 4 3 2 1

Contents

Who Was Jane Austen?

Every year, *People* magazine publishes a special issue. The magazine focuses on the twenty-five most interesting people 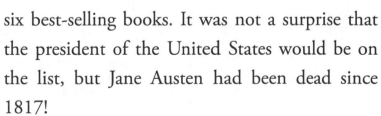 of the year. In 1995, their list included President Bill Clinton; Brad Pitt, one of the world's most famous movie stars; Princess Diana, the "people's princess"; and Jane Austen, the author of six best-selling books. It was not a surprise that the president of the United States would be on the list, but Jane Austen had been dead since 1817!

But in 1995, several very popular TV miniseries and movies based on her books had premiered. Why would books that were published so long ago be so popular two hundred years later? Perhaps it was because Jane Austen's characters were smart, funny, and very entertaining—even into the twentieth and twenty-first centuries. Readers in the 1800s felt a connection to the

people in her books. And people today still feel as if they know her characters personally.

Jane Austen created books about regular people and their everyday struggles and triumphs. She proved that ordinary characters and the drama of their daily lives could sometimes make the most interesting stories.

CHAPTER 1
Off to School

Reverend George Austen looked after the parish in Steventon, a small village about fifty miles west of London. He and his wife, Cassandra, had expected their seventh child to be born in November. But the baby did not arrive until December 16, 1775. They named her Jane.

In the south of England, the winter of 1775 was very cold and snowy. The harsh weather kept the Austen children inside. But Jane's siblings—James, George, Edward, Henry, Cassandra, and Francis—were happy to have another baby to play with. And the Austens were pleased that Cassandra, who was almost three years old, now had a sister.

Once spring arrived in Steventon, Jane was sent to live with a foster family in the village. Sending a baby to live with another family might sound strange, but this was common at the time. All of Jane's brothers and sisters had also gone to live with other families when they were young. Jane's parents felt it would be easier for their youngest children to return home when they were older, especially since the house was already very crowded.

Reverend Austen also used the family home—which was called a rectory—as a school. He tutored students to earn money to support his family.

Steventon Rectory

From August to December and February to June, the Austens had students living with them. Reverend Austen taught them Latin, Greek, geography, and science. The students, who were all boys, slept in the attic rooms at the top of the house. Jane's father also raised cows, sheep, and chickens to bring in extra money to support his growing family.

By the time Jane was three years old, she was once again living with her family, and her younger brother, Charles, had been born. In 1779, Thomas Knight, a wealthy cousin, visited the Austen family with his wife, Catherine. The Knights were charmed by Jane's brother Edward, who was twelve at the time. The couple asked if Edward could join them on their travels. And in 1783, the Knights officially adopted Edward, who became the heir to their large fortune. That meant that someday he would inherit the Knights' money and their property.

Thomas Knight

The Austens' house was crowded and noisy. But although they did not have a lot of money, it was a happy, comfortable place. The library was filled with Reverend Austen's books, and Jane spent a lot of time reading there. The family also read out loud to one another. And Jane's parents encouraged their children and Reverend Austen's students to write and to put on skits—short performances for their own entertainment.

Georgian England

The years between 1714 and 1830 in England are called the *Georgian Period*. This is because during this time, Kings George I, George II, George III, and George IV ruled the country.

Life improved for many people during these years. The discovery of new medicines meant that certain diseases were kept under control. The invention of new farming methods and equipment made farms more productive. And the Industrial Revolution created an increase in manufacturing and trade.

Although most people still lived and worked in the countryside, many began moving to towns and cities. People in the middle class, whether they lived in the country or the city, now had more free time to enjoy hobbies such as gardening, reading, writing, and music.

At the time, it was not common to send girls to school. Most people thought that was a waste of time and money. Girls learned to sew, sing, and play music. They were expected to focus on having good manners, getting married, and preparing to be good wives when they grew up.

But Jane's older sister, Cassandra, was sent to a boarding school in Oxford in the spring of 1783 when she was ten years old. Jane and her older sister had become very good friends, and Jane begged her parents to let her go to boarding school as well.

Soon after the girls arrived, Mrs. Cawley, who ran the school, moved it to Southampton, a town on the south coast of England. Although Jane—who was now seven years old—was with Cassandra, she hated the school. She found it too serious and stern compared to the school her father ran in their home back in Steventon. Jane also missed the freedom she had in the countryside.

Southampton was a busy port city at the time. Many soldiers returning from their duties overseas landed there. Some of these soldiers came home with typhoid fever—a dangerous infection.

The disease spread quickly through the city, and both Cassandra and Jane became very sick. Mrs. Cawley did not tell Reverend and Mrs. Austen that their daughters were ill.

But the girls' cousin Jane Cooper also attended the same school. She wrote her mother a letter saying that Jane and Cassandra had typhoid fever. As soon as the Austens heard the news, Mrs. Austen rushed to Southampton. She cared for her daughters until they were well enough to return home.

Jane and Cassandra spent the next year at home studying with Reverend Austen. Their father let the girls read any of the almost five hundred books in his library. Jane read plays, classic poetry, and humorous novels.

In 1785, the Austens decided to send their daughters back to school. They wanted them to continue their education at the Abbey School in Reading. Again, their cousin Jane Cooper joined them. The school had a good reputation, and the Austen sisters and their cousin were happy there. The girls had classes in the morning and their afternoons were free.

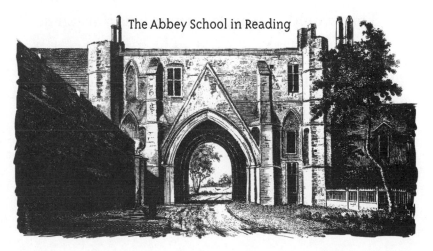
The Abbey School in Reading

But it was getting difficult to pay the tuition. The Austens decided to bring Jane and Cassandra back home.

That would be the last time Jane Austen set foot in a school. Her formal education had ended, and she was just eleven years old. Jane would never spend much time away from her family again.

CHAPTER 2
Watching and Listening

Jane was glad to be back home. Once again she had the freedom to take long walks in the countryside. Steventon was a lot less noisy and busy than either Southampton or Reading had been. But Jane enjoyed the buzz and activity in her family's home. She joined in when her father's students put on skits. She also decided to start writing.

Over Christmastime in 1786, Jane's cousin Eliza Hancock, who was fourteen years older than Jane, visited the Austens. Eliza was the beautiful daughter of Reverend Austen's sister, Philadelphia. Eliza was married to a French count, which made her a countess. Her stories of life in France dazzled Jane. Eliza loved music and drama, and she joined the funny shows that the family put on. Jane thought Eliza was like a character from the novels on her father's bookshelves.

Eliza visited the Austens again at the end of 1787. She continued to fascinate twelve-year-old Jane with her stories about life in France and the famous people she had met. Eliza also rented a piano so that the Austens could play music and dance at home. She gave Jane books in French and encouraged her to learn the language.

Eliza's exciting life inspired Jane to write even more stories. Most of them were about thieves, murderers, or people who had no common sense. Many of her characters escaped ridiculous situations or horrible accidents. Jane always read her humorous stories aloud to her family.

Jane's early writing sometimes made fun of novels that were popular at the time. Jane felt that many of the female characters in these novels were too silly or sentimental. She didn't like to read novels about women who were worried about only one thing: finding a rich husband. The women that Jane knew were all strong and independent. She felt that couples should marry because they were in love, not to increase the size of their bank accounts.

One of the most popular novels, which Jane *did* like, was called *Cecilia* by Fanny Burney. In the book, the main character, Cecilia Beverley,

Frances "Fanny" Burney

is told that she must marry a man who agrees to

take her last name, rather than change her own name after marriage. This causes all kinds of confusion among Cecilia's family and friends.

The idea of a man using his wife's last name was simply ridiculous in the 1780s. It was not

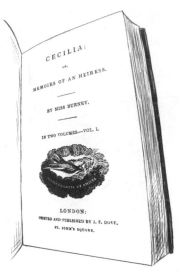

an easy task, and Cecilia's inheritance depended on it. Cecilia ended up losing most of her money. Near the end of the story, one of the characters says, "The whole of this unfortunate business . . . has been the result of PRIDE AND PREJUDICE." This meant that people sometimes make unfortunate decisions based on keeping up appearances and always following the rules.

Jane already had plenty of people and things to write about. But in 1788, when she was thirteen

The Modern Novel

Today, over sixty thousand novels—long fictional stories—are published in the United States every year. But in the 1800s, this kind of book wasn't very common. Up until this time, books were mostly about history, religion, or mythology. They were often written in poetic verse, such as the *Odyssey* by Homer and Chaucer's *Canterbury Tales*.

Novels that became popular in England at this time were tales of adventure, often in far-off places. They were written in a style that was easy to read and understand. Two of the most popular were *Robinson Crusoe* by Daniel Defoe and *The History of Tom Jones, A Foundling* by Henry Fielding.

years old, Jane and her family visited relatives in London. The exciting sights and sounds of England's largest city captured her imagination. Jane came home with lots of ideas for new stories. She called one of them *Love and Freindship* (Jane spelled it incorrectly). Jane dedicated it to her cousin Eliza. The story is full of carriage crashes,

robberies, and eloping couples. Jane was making fun of the romantic novels that were being published at the time. She laughed at the women in novels who had very little common sense. Her two main characters in *Love and Freindship*, Laura and Sophia, were always fainting.

Jane wrote her work in three different notebooks. They are called the *Juvenilia*, meaning stories from her youth. They contain stories, dramatic scenes, and an original history of England, which Cassandra illustrated. Jane's writing, and her cherished notebooks, were very important to her. Even though some of her stories were funny and at times even silly, Jane was taking her work seriously.

CHAPTER 3
Changes

Jane and her siblings were growing up, and their lives were changing. James had become a minister like their father and had married Anne Mathew. Edward had married Elizabeth Bridges and had moved to Kent. Henry was studying at Oxford University. Reverend and Mrs. Austen wanted Henry to become a minister, too. But when war broke out between England and France in 1793, Henry left college and joined the army. Francis was a sailor away on duty. And Charles was a student at the Royal Naval Academy in Portsmouth.

The Royal Naval Academy

Jane's second-oldest brother, George, was almost ten years older than she was. He had difficulty speaking and hearing and may have been completely deaf and unable to speak. The Austens were not able to give George the care he needed, so he was sent to live with foster parents.

Most of Jane's brothers were off doing exciting things. But Jane and her sister were still living in Steventon with their parents. Teenage Jane and Cassandra did the things that young women were expected to do—sew, read, visit friends, and play music. Jane also continued to write and fill her notebooks with stories.

Jane and Cassandra were now old enough to attend dances and dinner parties. They were also the right age to start looking for husbands.

The Austen sisters were invited to many dances and parties. They were both smart, attractive young women with good manners.

People liked having them as guests. Jane was tall and had hazel eyes, bright pink cheeks, and brown hair that curled around her face. The Austen sisters were also good dancers.

Jane's brother Henry said that Jane "was fond of dancing and excelled in it . . . her carriage and deportment were quiet, yet graceful."

Manydown

Jane and Cassandra attended several dances at the beautiful estate called Manydown Park. This was the home of the wealthy Bigg family, who had moved to Steventon in 1789. The Austen sisters were close friends of Catherine, Elizabeth, and Alethea Bigg, and their brother, Harris.

The balls and social events that Jane attended gave her even more material for her stories.

She continued to watch and listen carefully to the young people around her. Men and women were supposed to behave in a certain way when they were together. They had to use their best, most formal manners.

Jane didn't like how most young women were expected to find a rich husband. It was a woman's goal to attract a wealthy man and marry him because of his money. It was not really important if she loved him. Because of this,

men always seemed to have the advantage. Jane thought it was sad to build a relationship on anything other than love.

In her writing, Jane commented on all the details of the party guests she met. After one dance where she had spoken with three sisters, Jane told Cassandra, "I was as civil to them as their bad breath would allow me!" At the time, many people may have thought these things, but they never would have talked about them or written them down. But Jane was never afraid to say what she thought.

Jane continued to write stories based on the people she met and the events she attended. The more she wrote, the better she got at it. Her early stories usually made fun of people and were full of exaggerated, silly situations. But as Jane grew up, so did her style of writing. Her new stories were much more realistic. One of Jane's nieces called them "inbetweenities, when the nonsense was passing away and before her wonderful talent had found its proper channel."

During this time, Cassandra had fallen in love with a man named Thomas Fowle. He had been one of Reverend Austen's students.

Even though Thomas did not make a lot of money as a minister, the Reverend and Mrs. Austen felt it was good match. Cassandra and Thomas were engaged in the winter of 1792. Thomas had been promised a better job in a wealthier parish as soon as it was available. So Cassandra and Thomas decided to wait to marry until Thomas was able to start his new position.

As with everything else, Jane was eager to do whatever Cassandra did—even get engaged!

Jane daydreamed a lot about getting married. She even made up marriages for herself and wrote them down, as if they were real, in the parish register at her father's church. Jane gave a few of her imaginary husbands names like "Henry Frederic Howard Fitzwilliam of London" and "Edmund Arthur William Mortimer of Liverpool." She later decided that her husband should have a name that wasn't so ridiculous.

So she changed the name in the register to simply "Jack Smith" and her own name to "Jane Smith late Austen."

But Jane was better at creating imaginary husbands on the page than she was at finding one in real life.

CHAPTER 4
A Romance of Her Own

On Jane's nineteenth birthday, her father gave her a small writing desk and a supply of writing paper and ink. Paper was expensive at this time, so the gift showed that Jane's father believed in his daughter's talent. He felt that Jane could be an author and make a living as a writer. Reverend Austen wanted Jane to have something to do other than worry about finding a husband.

Jane now had a place to write. But, unfortunately, she often had to put her writing aside. In early 1794, Eliza's husband, the French count, was put to death in France. As a wealthy noble, he was one of the many victims of the French Revolution. The people leading the revolution wanted to do away with the royalty (their king and queen) and the noble families who were close to them.

Eliza was suddenly a widow. She was also broke. The French revolutionaries had seized her husband's estate, so she stayed with the Austens for several months. Eliza found great comfort with her family.

The French Revolution, 1789–1799

Louis XVI

In 1789, the French people rebelled against their king—Louis XVI—and the noble classes. They were tired of having to pay taxes that supported the fancy lifestyles of the richest French citizens. On July 14, 1789, the revolutionaries stormed a prison in Paris called the Bastille, hoping to collect weapons and ammunition. They formed a new government called the National Constituent Assembly.

For the next ten years, there was a struggle in France as different groups tried to gain control of the country. Some people still wanted to have a king. But others wanted a democracy, in which every person would be represented in the government. The revolution finally ended when Napoleon Bonaparte took control of and established a new system of government—the Consulate.

Napoleon

In May 1795, James's wife died very suddenly. Their daughter, Anna, was only two years old at the time. James was overcome with sadness at the death of his wife. He didn't think he would be able to look after his parish and his daughter. James asked his mother and his sisters to help. So for the next two years, Jane's niece Anna lived at home with the Austens.

But Jane still made time to write even though her family needed her help. She was working on her first novel. The title was *Elinor and Marianne*. It was the story of two sisters told through a series of letters that the sisters write to each other.

Marianne was very emotional. She couldn't wait to fall in love and get married. Her older sister, Elinor, was just the opposite: practical, patient, and in no rush to get married.

In January 1796, Jane wrote a letter to Cassandra, who was visiting her future in-laws. Jane told her sister that she had met a charming, handsome young man at a ball. The young man was named Thomas Lefroy. He was Irish and had recently moved to the area. The day after the ball, Thomas had visited Jane at home. They talked about many things, including their favorite books.

Thomas Lefroy

Jane and Thomas continued to meet. At the time, however, a young woman was not supposed to spend time alone with a young man. It wasn't considered the proper thing to do.

Jane and Thomas's private meetings were soon discovered, and Thomas was teased about it. Jane was in love with Thomas, but their relationship was attracting attention.

Thomas Lefroy's family heard about their son's affection for Jane. They had wanted him to marry someone from a wealthy family. They did not want their son to fall in love with a minister's daughter. Thomas's parents quickly sent him to London to study law. Jane was heartbroken.

She thought that Thomas might ask her to marry him. But Jane never saw or heard from Thomas again.

Jane poured her sadness about the end of her relationship with Thomas Lefroy into her writing. She was not happy with *Elinor and Marianne*, so she started a new novel called *First Impressions*. Jane wanted her main character to be strong and smart. In the story, the character Elizabeth Bennett enjoyed reading, having intelligent conversations with family and friends, and she always spoke her mind. She didn't like silly women who were weak and felt like they needed a man to help them make decisions. Jane had based Elizabeth on herself and her sister.

Jane enjoyed working on *First Impressions*. She felt more confident about it than she had about *Elinor and Marianne*. But just when Jane was starting to be truly happy again, Cassandra received some bad news. She had been looking

forward to her marriage once Thomas Fowle
returned from the West Indies. But in the spring
of 1797, Cassandra learned that Tom had died of
yellow fever earlier in the year.

Jane and Cassandra had always been close. But the sadness that they felt over lost love brought them even closer together. They had both been in love, but the romances were not to be.

Jane worked hard on *First Impressions* and finished the manuscript later in the year. She was just twenty-one years old. Reverend Austen had read all of Jane's work, and so he read *First Impressions*, too. He was impressed by his daughter's novel. He decided to send it to a publishing company in London. But Jane's father did not tell the publisher who the author was. Jane's manuscript was returned with a note that read "declined by Return of Post." Jane was upset. The novel that she and her family felt was so well written had been rejected. But Jane would not give up. She was determined to have her work published.

CHAPTER 5
A New Home

By early 1798, Jane was very busy. She decided that writing *Elinor and Marianne* as a series of letters was too complicated. Jane rewrote the book with paragraphs, chapters, and conversations between the characters. And then she decided that the novel needed a new title. She renamed it *Sense and Sensibility*.

In the summer of 1798, Jane, Cassandra, and their parents went to visit Edward and his family. Edward and his wife, Elizabeth, now had four children and lived in a large mansion called Godmersham. It was owned by his adoptive parents, the Knights. Jane was amazed by the grand house, the beautiful gardens, and rolling hills of the large estate.

In October 1798, Jane and her parents returned home to Steventon. Elizabeth had asked Cassandra to stay and help take care of her and Edward's infant son.

Mrs. Austen became ill when they returned home, and Jane had to look after her mother and the rest of the household. While it was Jane's duty to help her family, she was jealous of Cassandra.

Her sister was living in a large, beautiful home with servants. And Jane was even more annoyed because Cassandra took such a long time to reply to Jane's letters! The sisters had always counted on each other for news. They also shared their most private thoughts and feelings. But now Jane felt that Cassandra was too busy with her new life.

Jane's brother James had remarried after his first wife died. His new wife was Mary Lloyd. James and Mary's first son was born in 1798.

At this point, Edward and Elizabeth had five children. Jane was happy to have nieces and nephews. But she was not content being an aunt. She was sad that she did not have a family of her own. Jane was now twenty-two. She was still young enough to get married, but her chances of meeting a husband seemed to be getting slim. How would she support herself if she didn't have a husband? Jane knew that it was more important than ever for her writing to help her earn a living.

In the spring of 1799, Cassandra returned to Steventon and once again took over the running of the house. Jane was happy to not have to do all the housework herself. In May,

Edward invited Jane and Mrs. Austen to travel to the town of Bath with him. He had been ill, and he hoped the waters of the spa there would help.

Jane was excited to visit Bath. Her latest novel, *Susan*, was about a wealthy woman who lived there. But it turned out that Jane did not like Bath.

She thought it was a crowded, noisy town full of snobs! After five weeks, Jane and her mother returned to Steventon.

For the next year, Jane's life followed a happy routine. She visited friends, took long walks in the country, helped her parents around the house, and continued to write. She even had time to finish her novel. Cassandra spent most of that year at Godmersham with Edward and his family. But this time, Jane's letters to her sister were not mean or jealous. Jane seemed to be happy with her life in Steventon.

In November 1800, Reverend Austen decided to retire. He broke the news by announcing, "Well, girls, it is all settled; we have decided to leave Steventon in such a week and go to Bath." Jane fainted when she heard the news! Jane had not enjoyed her time in Bath at all. She loved the woods and fields that surrounded Steventon.

But Jane was not married, and she did not have a job. In 1800, young women who were not married relied on their families for money and a place to live. They were not allowed to live alone. Jane had no choice but to move with her parents to the town of Bath. Maybe it was this shocking, sudden change that made her even more determined to become a published author.

CHAPTER 6
A Proposal

At the start of the new year, Jane and her parents were busy preparing for the move to their new home. Reverend Austen decided to sell most of the family's furniture, including Jane's piano. He also sold many of the books in the library and all the painted scenery from the Austen family's plays. He planned to buy new furniture when they arrived in Bath.

Jane and her mother arrived in Bath in May 1801 and began looking for a house to rent. Reverend Austen and Cassandra would join them in June. Jane was still unhappy about the move. In a letter to Cassandra, she wrote, "Another stupid party last night . . . with six people to look on and talk nonsense to each other." Jane was having trouble starting over in a new place and meeting new friends in Bath.

At this point, Jane had written three novels, and she wanted to write more. But while the family lived in Bath, Jane hardly wrote at all. She rarely sat at her desk and picked up her pen. Jane needed the calmness of the countryside to write. She missed the peace and quiet where she could dream up stories and characters.

Now that Reverend Austen was retired, the family spent much of their time traveling. They visited towns on the southern coast of England, where they took walks on the beach.

And they also visited Edward and his family at Godmersham. At the end of 1802, Jane and Cassandra went to visit their old friends the Bigg family at Manydown Park. The house had many memories for Jane. This is where she had fallen in love with Tom Lefroy. Jane was looking forward to spending time with her friends Catherine, Alethea, and Elizabeth Bigg. She was happy to get away from Bath and be back in a beautiful home surrounded by fields and forests.

The Bigg sisters'
younger brother, Harris,
was also at Manydown.
Jane remembered him
as an awkward young
boy. But he was now
a tall young man.
And as the only son,
he would inherit the
family's large fortune
when his father died.

Harris Bigg-Wither

His family was eager for him to find a wife. So on
December 2, 1802, he proposed to Jane. She was
twenty-six and Harris was twenty-one.

This seemed like a good match for Jane.
Marrying Harris would give her security and a
comfortable life. When Harris inherited the estate
of Manydown, Cassandra would be able to come
live with her sister. Jane said "yes" to Harris.

But by the morning of December 3, Jane had

changed her mind. She and Cassandra had sat up most of the night talking about the proposal. Jane realized marrying Harris would be a mistake. She did not love him. Although many women at that time married the wealthiest man who might ask them, or out of a sense of duty to their family, Jane wanted to marry for love. She said, "I consider everybody as having a right to marry *once* in their Lives for Love."

Jane let Harris know that she had changed her mind. Then she and Cassandra quickly left Manydown and went home to Bath. Jane returned to her writing.

More than ever, she still hoped to become a published author. If she could not find her true love, she would have to rely on her talent to earn a living. With the help of her brother Henry, Jane sold the manuscript for her novel *Susan* to a London publisher named Richard Crosby. He paid about $1,000 in today's money for the

rights to publish her novel. This was almost a
year's salary! Mr. Crosby promised Henry that he
would publish the book quickly.

The Role of Women in Georgian England

During Jane Austen's lifetime, women had very limited—and sometimes no—rights regarding possessions or property. If they were married, everything they owned belonged to their husbands. And if they were single, everything belonged to their father.

A woman was expected to be good at playing music, dancing, and conversation. She learned the proper ways of behaving and was expected to use her best manners at all times.

Many families expected their daughters to find husbands who would improve their family's wealth and status. The idea of marrying for love was far less important.

CHAPTER 7
Independence

Although selling her manuscript gave Jane new energy to keep writing, family matters became much more important. Reverend Austen had not been well since the family moved to Bath. At the end of 1804 and early in 1805, Jane's father felt ill once again. The family sent for a doctor. But he could not help Jane's father's fever. Reverend Austen died on January 21, 1805.

Jane, her mother, and her sister were very sad about the death of Reverend Austen. They were now also worried about their own futures. According to the custom of the time, James, the eldest son, would inherit his father's estate. The Austen women had no money of their own.

They would have to rely on the generosity of Jane's brothers. And they could not continue living in Bath.

For the next year, Jane, Cassandra, and their mother moved from place to place. They stayed with family and friends who were kind enough to take them in. They visited James and Mary in Steventon, Edward and Elizabeth in Godmersham, and Francis and his new wife, Mary, in Southampton.

Jane was glad to leave Bath behind, but she was frustrated by this kind of life. She was constantly packing and unpacking her bags, and she was not able to write. Jane wanted a place to call home. She wanted a place where she could write.

Edward's wife, Elizabeth, died in October 1808, after giving birth to their eleventh child. Cassandra had come to help with the birth, and she stayed on at Godmersham to help run the house after Elizabeth died. Even with Cassandra's help,

Edward struggled to look after all his children. So he sent two of his sons to visit their Aunt Jane at Francis and Mary's house in Southampton. The young boys were grief stricken at the loss of their mother. But Jane kept them busy and made sure they had plenty to do. She played games with them, took them to see a battleship being built, and floated paper boats on the river. She made up riddles to entertain them.

Edward had not given his mother and sisters much money when Reverend Austen died. But Jane's kindness to his sons changed his mind. He gave them something they hadn't had since they left Steventon almost nine years earlier—a home of their own. Edward offered his mother and sisters the choice of two properties he had inherited from the Knights. One was near Godmersham. The other was in the village of Chawton, in the beautiful countryside of Hampshire. The women chose the house in Chawton.

Mrs. Austen and her daughters felt a huge sense of relief. They would no longer have to depend on their relatives for a place to stay. They would have their own home in the country. It would provide Jane with the peace and quiet she needed to write. She would have her own room where she could continue to work.

It had now been almost six years since her brother had sold the rights to *Susan* to Richard Crosby. Jane wrote to him saying that if she didn't hear back, she would send the manuscript to another publisher. Because Mr. Crosby had never known the author's name, Jane called herself Mrs. Ashton Dennis. She used only initials and signed the letter "M.A.D." Richard Crosby wrote back to say that he would return the manuscript to her if she repaid the money he had paid for it. But Jane no longer had it. What money she had left was spent paying the household bills. So Jane was unable to buy back the manuscript. Her novel remained unpublished, but owned by Richard Crosby.

CHAPTER 8
Success at Last

Jane's new home in Chawton was a redbrick, two-story building. It had been built in the 1700s as an inn. The house was close to a busy road that many coaches used to travel between London and Southampton. It had six bedrooms, two parlors,

and attic rooms—called *garrets*—that could be used for storage or as bedrooms for servants. The Chawton house also had a large garden with fruit trees, vegetables, flowers, and a pond.

Jane and her mother were the first to move into the house in July 1809. Shortly after moving in, Jane wrote a note to her brother Frank:

Our Chawton home, how much we find
Already in it, to our mind;
And how convinced, that when complete
It will all other Houses beat
That ever have been made or mended,
With rooms concise, or rooms distended.
You'll find us very snug next year.

Jane was now thirty-three years old. She had accepted the fact that she would probably never get married. She also accepted the fact that her novel *Susan* might never be published. But Jane was happier than she had been in a long, long time. The new home was comfortable. And it was in the countryside that Jane loved so much. There were lots of paths and trails. Jane took walks and thought about revising the novels she had already written. And she was inspired with ideas for new books, too.

Life in Chawton fell into a routine for Jane, and it was a routine she enjoyed. She woke up and practiced the piano before making breakfast for everyone. She would then sew or embroider and make shopping trips to the village. She played with her nieces and nephews when they visited— all seventeen of them! Jane also continued to write. She had a small writing desk in the parlor where the piano was.

During 1809 and 1810, Jane decided to revise *Sense and Sensibility*. Once she was happy with it, Jane sent the manuscript to a different publisher,

Thomas Egerton. He liked the book, but he did not want to take a risk on an unknown writer, especially a woman. Egerton told Jane that he would publish the book if she paid the cost of printing it herself. Jane was determined to see one of her books published. Her brother Henry knew how important this was to Jane, so he and his wife, Eliza, agreed to pay for *Sense and Sensibility* to be printed.

It took a long time for a book to be published in the 1800s. The type was put in place letter by letter, and the paper press was turned by hand.

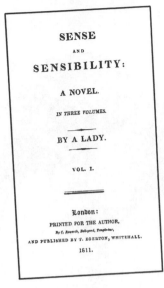

The printing began in April, but the book didn't appear in stores until October 1811. Because it was not considered proper for women to earn money by writing, Jane's name didn't appear in the book. The author was listed simply as "A Lady." But that didn't bother Jane. Finally, one of her stories would be read by more people than just her family.

Sense and Sensibility received good reviews. One said the author had "much knowledge of character" and "a great deal of good sense." Another said the book was "well written, highly pleasing, interesting" with an "entertaining narrative." They praised the "unknown" author's story about Elinor and Marianne's struggles to find love as the events of their lives unfolded around them.

By July 1813, every printed copy of *Sense and Sensibility* had been sold. Jane earned what would be nearly $15,000 in today's money!

Because *Sense and Sensibility* had done so well, Thomas Egerton offered to publish Jane's next book. And she had the manuscript for *First Impressions* ready for him. But a book had already been published with that title. Jane remembered one of her favorite lines from *Cecilia* by Fanny Burney, and she called her new book *Pride and Prejudice*.

Mr. Egerton paid Jane more than ten times what Richard Crosby had paid for *Susan*! *Pride and Prejudice* was published in January 1813. Once again, the title page didn't reveal Jane's name. It read only "By the Author of *Sense and Sensibility*."

The book was 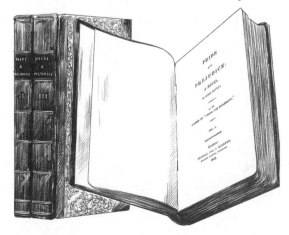 so popular that a second printing was scheduled for later the same year.

A Comedy of Manners

Pride and Prejudice is an example of a comedy of manners. This style of writing describes—and often makes fun of—the manners and lifestyles of fashionable and wealthy people. In the 1800s, people were expected to be so polite and well-mannered that they often appeared to be exactly the opposite: awkward and artificial.

In the novel—just like in real life at that time—the characters find themselves doing and saying what they feel they *must*, rather than what they truly *want*. And Jane Austen knew how to find the humor in the most "proper" situations.

Finally, Jane's writing was being taken seriously! Her next book was called *Mansfield Park*. Jane finished writing it in July 1813, and it was published in May 1814. *Mansfield Park* was written when Jane was thirty-seven years old. Although she was still writing about the drama surrounding the search for the right husband, Jane now looked at marriage as serious business. Her writing was much less comical.

Because *Mansfield Park* was more serious than her other books and the main character is plain and shy, Mr. Egerton was worried that it wouldn't sell as well. So he made the same deal with Henry Austen as he had for Jane's first novel. He agreed to publish the book as long as Jane paid for the printing costs. Jane confidently agreed. She felt that readers connected with the honest stories she told, and she hoped that this book would be as successful as her first two had been.

CHAPTER 9
The Words Live On

While the manuscript for *Mansfield Park* was being set at the printer, Jane began her fourth novel, *Emma*. The story of *Emma* was funny and lighthearted, more in the style of her first two books. Jane said she wanted to  create a strong female character "whom no one but myself will much like." The book focuses on Emma's attempts at matchmaking—setting her friends up on dates—which all end in disaster.

Mansfield Park was a success and the first printing sold out within six months. Jane earned more money than she had ever earned before. But Mr. Egerton refused to reprint the book! This upset Henry Austen. Because no one knew that Jane was the author, her brother Henry contacted another publisher on Jane's behalf. He sold *Emma* to John Murray in December 1815. Mr. Murray also bought the rights to publish *Mansfield Park* and *Sense and Sensibility*.

Henry became ill in November, and Jane stayed with him while he recovered. One of the doctors who came to visit Henry was the personal physician to the Prince of Wales—the son of King George III and the heir to the throne of England.

While treating Henry, the doctor told Jane that the Prince of Wales enjoyed reading her books!

Jane was invited to visit the prince's library at Carlton House in London. While she was there, the librarian suggested that she dedicate her next book to the prince. Jane was shocked by this request. The prince was known for his selfishness and sometimes scandalous behavior. Jane did not want to mention him in her book.

But Jane's family told her that she could not turn down this request. Dedicating her book to the prince might help sell more copies. So

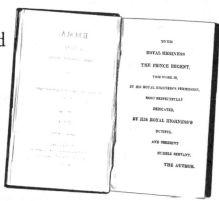

Jane agreed and dedicated *Emma* to the Prince of Wales. She also presented him with a special red-leather bound copy.

Most critics agreed that *Emma* was Jane's best book yet. Sir Walter Scott, a famous author at that time, said that *Emma* was a great example of a new style of novel that showed ordinary people and everyday life.

But there was still one manuscript of Jane's that had not been published. So Jane asked Henry to get in touch with Richard Crosby and buy back the rights to *Susan*. It had now been thirteen years since he had paid so little for the manuscript he never published. Once Henry made the deal, he told the publisher that *Susan* was by the same author of the very successful books *Pride and Prejudice*, *Sense and Sensibility*, *Mansfield Park*, and *Emma*. Mr. Crosby had passed up a very big opportunity!

While she was writing her next book, Jane began to feel ill. She and Cassandra traveled to a spa, hoping that the rest and warm waters might help with Jane's fever and the pain in her back.

When they returned home to Chawton, Jane finished the first draft of her latest manuscript. There were parts she wanted to revise. But before she did, she decided to go back and once again work on *Susan*.

As the year went on, Jane began to feel better. She finished *Susan* and retitled it *Northanger Abbey*. And she also finished her new manuscript, which she called *Persuasion*. But not long into the new year of 1817, Jane's fever and pain returned.

It became too difficult for Jane to work, so she put her writing aside.

Jane tried to hide her illness. She joked about it in letters to her family. But she privately took it seriously enough to write her will in April 1817. She wanted to leave small gifts to her brother Henry and his housekeeper. Everything else she would leave to her "dearest Sister Cassandra." In May, Jane went to visit a new doctor. But it was clear that there was not much that could be done for her. Although she was growing weaker, Jane continued to have visitors and write letters to friends and family.

On July 18, 1817, at the age of forty-one, Jane Austen died. Cassandra was at her bedside. Six days later, Jane was buried in Winchester Cathedral, the city's ancient, historic church.

Jane's family knew how much her novels meant to her. After her death, they made sure that both *Northanger Abbey* and *Persuasion* were published. And for the first time, Jane's name appeared as the author of her books.

In 1869, her nephew, James Edward Austen-Leigh, published *A Memoir of Jane Austen*. The memoir introduced all six of Jane's novels to a much larger audience. Fifty-two years after her death, Jane Austen's writing was, once again, as popular as ever.

James Edward Austen-Leigh

Jane's *Juvenilia* notebooks still exist: One is in the Bodleian Library in Oxford, England, and the other two are in the British Museum in London. And her work lives on in countless adaptations: movies, television shows, and new versions of her beloved stories.

Jane Austen accomplished what she set out to do: She achieved success as a published author in a time when it was very uncommon for women to even dream of having careers. Although she was not famous during her lifetime, her novels have rarely been out of print since then.

And in 2013, the Bank of England announced that Jane Austen will be the first woman whose portrait will appear on British money. In addition to Jane's face, the ten-pound banknote will feature the following quote: "I declare after all there is no enjoyment like reading!"

"I declare after all there is no enjoyment like reading!"

On the Screen

These are just a few of the many movies and TV shows based on the Jane Austen novels *Pride and Prejudice*, *Sense and Sensibility*, *Mansfield Park*, *Emma*, *Northanger Abbey*, and *Persuasion*:

- **1940:** *Pride and Prejudice* (starring Laurence Olivier)
- **1983:** *Mansfield Park* (TV miniseries)
- **1995:** *Clueless* (starring Alicia Silverstone; based on *Emma*)

- **1995:** *Pride and Prejudice* (TV miniseries)
- **1995:** *Sense and Sensibility* (starring Emma Thompson and Kate Winslet)
- **1996:** *Emma* (starring Gwyneth Paltrow)

- 2001: *Bridget Jones's Diary* (starring Renée Zellweger; based on *Pride and Prejudice*)
- 2007: *Becoming Jane* (starring Anne Hathaway; based on Jane Austen's letters)
- 2007: *Northanger Abbey* (TV movie)

- 2016: *Love & Friendship* (starring Kate Beckinsale; based on the novella, *Lady Susan*)
- 2016: *Pride and Prejudice and Zombies* (starring Lily James)

Timeline of Jane Austen's Life

1775	Born in Steventon, England, on December 16
1785– 1786	Attends Abbey School in Reading, England
1783	Brother Edward adopted by Mr. and Mrs. Thomas Knight
1788	Travels to Kent and London with her sister, Cassandra, and their parents
1795	Begins writing *Elinor and Marianne*
1796	Begins writing *First Impressions*
1797	*First Impressions* rejected by publisher
	Retitles *Elinor and Marianne* as *Sense and Sensibility*
1798	Begins writing *Susan*
1801	Moves with family to Bath
1802	Receives marriage proposal from Harris Bigg-Wither, but declines
1809	Moves to Chawton Cottage with mother and sister, Cassandra
1811	*Sense and Sensibility* is published
	Retitles *First Impressions* as *Pride and Prejudice*
1813	*Pride and Prejudice* published
	Completes and sells *Mansfield Park*
1814	*Mansfield Park* is published
1815	*Emma* is published
	Finishes writing *Persuasion*
1817	Dies in Winchester, England, on July 18

Timeline of the World

1775	The American Revolution begins
1776	The Declaration of Independence is signed
1782	*Cecilia* by Fanny Burney is published
1792	The US Postal Service is created on February 20
1793	Eli Whitney invents the cotton gin
1795	Nicolas-Jacques Conté invents modern pencil lead
1796	Edward Jenner introduces vaccination against smallpox
1799	Rosetta stone found in Egypt
1803	Louisiana Territory purchased from France by the United States
1804	Napoleon proclaimed emperor in France
	The Lewis and Clark expedition begins
1809	Edgar Allan Poe is born
1812	The United States declares war on Great Britain
	Charles Dickens is born

The Works of Jane Austen

1811: *Sense and Sensibility* (originally titled *Elinor and Marianne*) is published

1813: *Pride and Prejudice* (originally titled *First Impressions*) is published

1814: *Mansfield Park* is published

1815: *Emma* is published

1817: *Northanger Abbey* (originally titled *Susan*) and *Persuasion* are published after Jane Austen's death

1871: *Lady Susan*, an unfinished novel written in 1793–1794, is published

1925: *Sanditon*, an unfinished novel written in 1817, is published

1933: *Juvenilia*, a collection of short stories and poems written in 1787–1793, is published

Bibliography

* Books for young readers

Byrne, Paula. *The Real Jane Austen: A Life in Small Things*. New York: Harper Perennial, 2014.

Halperin, John. *The Life of Jane Austen*. Baltimore: The Johns Hopkins University Press, 1996.

Le Faye, Deirdre. *The British Library Writers' Lives: Jane Austen*. New York: Oxford University Press, 2000.

* Reef, Catherine. *Jane Austen: A Life Revealed*. New York: Clarion Books, 2011.

* Ruth, Amy. *Jane Austen*. Minneapolis, MN: Lerner Publications Company, 2001.

* Wagner, Heather Lehr. *Who Wrote That?: Jane Austen*. New York: Chelsea House Publishers, 2004.

Websites

www.britannica.com/biography/Jane-Austen

www.biography.com/people/jane-austen-9192819

www.janeausten.org/

www.jasna.org/info/about_austen.html